THE LOVELINESS OF THIS WORLD

poems by

John L. Wright

Finishing Line Press
Georgetown, Kentucky

THE LOVELINESS OF THIS WORLD

DANCERS

On a stage of high ground
Midst a marshy meadow
Poplars
Clad in silver and green leaves
Or unclad to their bark-white skin
Dance with the wind.

ACKNOWLEDGMENTS

Fourteen poems in this collection have appeared in the following journals:

JAMA
The Journal of Medical Humanities
penwood review
The Pharos
The Avocet: a journal of nature poetry, and *The Weekly Avocet* (on-line)

Many of the other poems have appeared in one or more of my four self-published
books: *Through an Old Wooden Bowl* (1999), *As Though Praying: Poems from Decatur
Island* (2002), *The Beginning of Love* (2005) and *Bumping Against the Glass* (2014).

Although these poems surely arose from all of the fifty-four years it has been my
privilege to live and raise a family in the Edmonds-Woodway, community on the banks
of Puget Sound, they were written only after I retired from the medical profession in
1994. And, they would not have been made at all had I not discovered, in 1988, that I
had the makings of a poet. And even more certain, none of the above would have been
possible had Lanita, my wife of fifty-eight years, not been such a steady and loving
companion.

For Jack Coulehan, a fellow physician-poet, who encouraged my making of poems for
thirty years, and for Priscilla Long, my teacher and editor for over twenty years, I am
also grateful.

Publisher: Leah Maines
Editor: Christen Kincaid
Cover Art: Terry L. Olmsted
Author Photo: Terry L. Olmsted
Cover Design: Elizabeth Maines McCleavy

Printed in the USA on acid-free paper.
Order online: www.finishinglinepress.com
        also available on amazon.com

Author inquiries and mail orders:
Finishing Line Press
P. O. Box 1626
Georgetown, Kentucky 40324
U. S. A.

Table of Contents

RESURRECTION

Careless eyes, indifferent ears,
an impoverished heart,
it took me years to relish the eagle's
cascading call,
the flicker's chattering flight.
Even in my backwoods,
how long before I cherish the pink
petals of *Rosa woodsii?*
I've tramped this town for decades
oblivious of the licorice fern
high on the bark of big-leaf maples:
missing its old fronds rust in May,
shrivel in June, vanish in July's dry heat.
And then, unexpectedly,
as if mud slid off my eyes,
I see its fronds coil out
—as if from death,
in late October's morning rain,
its hidden roots running cool
beneath the darkest moss.

THE LOVELINESS OF THIS WORLD

I don't need my brother's birthright. I don't need a ladder heaven-ward, this world is the other world. I'm lying here on this humus-soft earth, my head resting on a smooth stone. I'm basking in a shaft of sun beaming down through hemlock, fir, and alder in which haloed mosquitos mill like unassigned angels, and higher yet, sun-made-colorless butterflies patrol like archangels scanning for schisms. Sated with the loveliness of this world, I don't need a larger store-barn either. Still, out of this ecstasy stands a question: who or what do I praise for making it so.

AFTER EONS OF EVOLUTION,
A MINOR DISAPPOINTMENT

Suddenly a hush.

The coyote stands
ten paces beyond the yew.
My dog, off leash, stays beside me.

A primal memory stirs:
the coyote almost speaks, almost
comes to us.

The dog barks.
The coyote lopes into the far woods.

A northern flicker
flies from the dying hemlock.

AUGUST STASIS

Brittle berries, off the native cherry,
crackle beneath the re-cycle bin
I'm rolling out the back drive flecked
with yellow leaves, remind me that
August stasis is an illusion.

E-mail trickles, pink lilies peak,
lady ferns begin their wilt, orange-
purple sunsets bore,
discount malls re-paint parking stripes,
even the American flag luffs dispassionately
over the post office.

But, like the tug-of-war within slack tide,
beneath this lull a battle rages.
The long light flooding spring and early summer
has run its course, and for two months
invisible levers have been bending the earth's axis
back toward night.

And then, this morning,
as if my heart had suddenly tilted,
these crackling red berries and dropped leaves
wake within me
the desire for darkness, cool rain,
the comfort of a flannel shirt.

THE BEGINNING OF LOVE
Father

Cedar stumps
old as you would be,
had your heart not carried you away,
stand sturdy, festooned
with wild huckleberry and salal.
Like tombstones,
they sanctify my chosen ground.

So you see,
I was taken aback that day
you poured kerosene on two stumps
and set them ablaze.

For years after your death,
I walked by those charred stumps
certain you did what you thought I needed:
back home we cleared hillsides of sumac
and scrub oak for fields of corn and wheat.

But this evening,
searching in my backwoods
I suddenly see:
I've become the man you feared I might,
a man for whom mankind is not dispersed,
bi-modally,
into the lost, into the found.

THE PORTUGAL LAUREL

At times I fear,
after decades of doctoring,
of stashing tears in the pockets
of a long white coat,
my soul has turned to salt.

Take for example, the Portugal Laurel.
It has graced the patio for thirty-five years,
grown up with the family, seen sorrows, joys.
It has provided shade and beauty,
following a morning rain it sparkles
in the afternoon sun, a million pieces
of dark green crystal, carnelian stems.
And many a midnight its branches
have hid the ashes of a sleepless cigar.

But now, children gone, the patio is a ruin.
The landscape architect proclaims
We need to open this space.
So yesterday I took the laurel down,
not the slightest hesitation. At the start
I was occupied by technical matters, how to
bring down a robust laurel safely,
how to dispose of it. Never mind the details,
but you know I had to use a chain saw,
the trunk was twelve inches at the base.
In an hour and a half it was gone, all except
the weeping stump.
Only then did I feel a single shiver of sadness.

And today? Well, today
I have this pale blue numbness
which I know by tomorrow
will be gone.

POETS PLAYING
for Jack and Anne

Never mind that my bridge is small,
that it crosses a stream of dry stones,
that it's painted Navajo red
—not orange-red as in Japanese gardens.

But when you suggest water lilies,
I offer Basho's frog. When you raise it
three koi, I up it one blue heron and,
over there by the native deer fern,

a golden full-moon maple. By now
we're laughing at this escalation,
our wives amused by poets playing,
freed for the moment of brooding concerns.

Never mind that my pond
is a failed patch of sod, that the bridge
does not lead to meditation furrows
raked in fine gravel, but to compost bins,

hidden behind a cedar log,
where the work of becoming is under way.
An act of nature that I now see
as the exact metaphor for hope.

DEAR ANNE

I write to tell you what you know:
it takes a lifetime
before prayers turn factual. So don't fret
that the leaf you prayed to and
dropped over the side of my small bridge
fell on a bed of dry stones.

That leaf will not carry a prayer
downstream to an open lake
nor to a sea under blue skies. That leaf
will sink into humus
dressing the floor of my back woods.

But last night I heard a barred owl hooting
and I wondered,
Could a leaf pass a prayer to an owl?
And then this morning an eagle,
its high-pitched falling notes, and I asked,
Would an owl pass a prayer to an eagle?

And just now, outside my window,
a hummingbird, its flashing ruby throat.

QUAILSONG

For weeks the quail have been calling.
Early morning and late afternoon
I hear their territorial song:
chi-ca'-go, chi-ca'-go, chi-ca'-go;

like the far whistle of a train
or the opening strains of Mahler's 9th
it compels me to slow my walk
or rest for a moment on a rake or a hoe.

These are California quail,
blue-gray feathers, a quivering plume,
their heads bobbing as they lead
a ragged line of chicks across the road.

The risk to their survival climbs
each time they scurry out into the open
in search of food and cover
think of the coyote, the hawk,
                                        the human.

ANNIVERSARY
for Lanita

Walking these woods we've lived in
for forty years,
I sometimes think of our life together,
of our love,
how it will never be whole, only
                              always arriving.

Still, this afternoon
the sky's right, the sun's guiding
patches of light
across the wood's plush carpet,
for one magic moment our love,
our life together, lifts
                              above all striving.

THREE WHITE FLOWERS
September, 2001

Named for its slithering rhizomes,
my snakeroot plant,
now in its second year, rises
four feet on six sturdy purple stalks.
Each stalk branches once or twice
opening into purple-green leaves
like hands raised in praise.

No flowers the first year, but just past
Labor Day, walking carefree in my yard,
I'm astonished by three white flowers:
tube brushes nodding on arched stems.

There will be fifteen flowers, rosettes
of tiny white petals on red-purple stems
bursting from a hundred purple buds.

I watch these fragile petals come and go
past the murderous crashes
on the World Trade Center, the Pentagon,
in a Pennsylvania field,
each petal transforms into one green seed.

And today, on the 24rd of September,
the day after the Flag returns to full mast,
I plant twenty-four blue crocuses,
each sprouting bulb four inches deep.

SURVIVAL

for Jean and Bob

Except for their white truck,
stuck in the driveway for six months,
and it's been weeks since we've seen them
on morning walks,
a neighbor might not suspect that cancer
is having its way in this house.

The lawn, blue-green of winter, is edged,
raked spotless.
Two sculpted Scotch pines,
a black bamboo, its tall stalks
tied to the northeast corner by rice twine
and by the entryway, a lace-leaf maple.

A cedar wreath,
festooned with pine cones and a red bow,
hangs on the front door.
And through the long evenings,
like a precisely crafted petition,
icicle lights dangle bright along the roof's clean gutter.

OTHERS
for Karen

Do you remember
painting clematis-like leaves
on light-switch covers?
It must be forty years ago—
long before you became
a wife and mother.

What were you thinking
when you picked up a brush
and leaned over a table?
Christmas gifts
for family and friends?

Years of cherished gifts
keeping the mosaic of others
echoing in our lives,
reminding us again and again
who we are.

CANINE ELEGIES

1

They were brothers, golden
retrievers from the same litter.
When they moved into our town
they had already beaten the odds,
moseying the roads, their coats
turned gray, patchy and dull.
I worried they'd be hit by a car,
the way their heads hung low
—looking neither right nor left,
two old men freed of all illusions.

*

What were they discussing?
Could one live without the other?
And the day did come when
only one meandered our lives.
Some say only man grieves loss,
but on the morning their mistress
had arranged a painless demise
for the bedfast one, she awoke
to find the walking one had died
quietly during the night.
I never did know their names.

2

He wears business on his face:
solemn, eyes focused straight on.
Or he is in some Oriental trance
whose depth I'll never fathom.
His blond, golden retriever,
equally disciplined, seemingly
content, is the only hint of
friendliness in this striding pair.
So I'm hesitant to enter their affair.
But it's early morning, and this is
a small town, so I always say, Hi.
And without turning his head
he mumbles a small recognition.

But this morning, he's walking
toward me without his dog.
So, without compunction, fearing
something's gone terribly wrong
I ask him, Where's your dog?
For the first time in three years
he stops, looks me in the eyes
and briefly shares our mutual fate:
he places the fingertips of his left
hand on his belly and says,
My friend's dog dying: Cancer.
My dog keeps her dog company.

PREDESTINATION
for David

See that Port Orford cedar.
Its growth determinants are as puzzling as yours
—known X dancing with unknown Y.
Unimpeded, its natural life
would have it thrive along the Oregon coast
where its trunk grows straight, and tough enough
to serve as masts on clipper ships.
But sometime after emerging, something,
I can't imagine what, obstructed its path—see how
it takes a horizontal, 360 degree detour.
Yet, like your return to the Gospels after briefly
straying through the wide gate,
for years now it has been growing as intended.
I call it David's tree.

IMMORTALITY AT SEVENTY-FIVE

Yesterday I noticed that my Japanese maple,
out by the front gate near an old hemlock, is not leafing
with its natural vigor. Its rear branches are dying.
I like it there with the landscape light on it.
I'll mulch around its roots, work in some fertilizer,
prune back the hemlock, water over summer.

Most mornings my wife and I walk our Labrador
three miles through this wooded town.
Not all is right around here, there are trees and shrubs
struggling where they don't belong.
But I like living here. I like gardening these two acres.
I'm grateful for this season of reborn senses.
For the wrong turns that led me here, I'm also grateful.

That red barn's a miniature of my grandfather's barn.
This shrug came from my father.
I like the idea of passing on more than chromosomes.
I like the idea of leaving bits of heaven for the next guy.
I like the idea of leaving bits of myself in poems.

I like going to the post office, too. Still...., why is it,
five days out of six, I'm so disappointed with the mail?

ONE WAY TO PRAISE

for Peter Ormsby, M.D. (1931-2005)

Between that empty champagne bottle collecting dust
on the library's top shelf
and those two opened bottles of wine waiting with four
crystal goblets on a stone table,
you and I have been friends for forty merciful years.

We knew that cancer had worn you thin,
that you were considering more chemo. Ann said you
ate everything but not much.
So Lanita prepared for lunch, corn chowder, fruit salad,
warm rolls and powder-sugar-dusted cookies.

But by then you were too weak to travel
the five miles between our magical gardens. I wanted
to tell you, Peter, how I waited too long,
and the champagne you gave me for looking after Ann
turned to vinegar, how I admired you
                    for praising each day with a boutonniere.

YELLOW DAFFODILS IN AN ORANGE VASE
for Ann

Still dark. I pour juice, make coffee.

On the glass-top table, cut flowers in a vase,
your gift to us after we had honored Peter's life.

I think of you—the abyss between expecting him
to appear for breakfast and knowing that he'll not.

My wife enters in a mauve robe and blue slippers.
She pours coffee. I turn to the morning paper.

MERCY

Take for example the Indian plum:
it doesn't boast that it's the first native shrub
wakening from winter sleep,
nor does it see itself, this first week in March,
with its lacy white blossoms
and chartreuse leaves, a crystal chandelier,
nor does it claim that bearing bittersweet
fruit for squirrels and songbirds
is its salvation, yet,
this morning, when winter darkness
with its ceaseless drizzle has me crying *Uncle*,
its rebirth becomes for me
a tangible mercy.

ORGANIC PRAYER

As a leaf sinks
layer by layer:
litter
duff
humus

So my prayers:
praise
gratitude
primitive groans

Return
on tender tips
of wood fern fronds

CHEMISTRY
for Avery

Wanting acceptance, the eighty-year-old gardener
leads the six-year-old girl past
white azaleas and magenta bleeding hearts
to his perennial garden.
There he pinches off an orange primrose flower dense
with fragrant molecules
and sets it on her finger. She lifts the flower to her nose
and shyly smiling sends a message that he
codes and files in his *Life is sweet, o so sweet* directory.

HALF-MAN STONES

I'm not talking mythology here—Centaur
Minotaur nor Sphinx.

I'm parsing the life of an eighty-year-old
who a decade-plus-ago raised,

with sturdy back and strong limbs,
a three-tiered stone wall using one-man

river basalt. A man who today
can barely wrestle *half*-man stones

into a two-tiered wall.
Still, he does not shrug. Behind the wall

he plants fragrant shrubs
and a flowering cherry,

his weightless-self continuing
to embroider an earthbound heaven.

THE WESTERN RED CEDAR

We've been conversing forty-seven years.
I've done the talking, but you, in silent green,
nearly symmetrical, have been the teacher:
There is a jagged line running through nature.
In the fall tips of your limbs become
rusty warning flags—cut your losses O man.
Upright for a century, you are a model
of patience, tirelessly scrubbing the air.

Can you have noticed or cared
that you've shut out the sun, that there's
an absence of flowers on my shrubs and vines?
Yet, while you still lived, I swear
I never once thought of your end as profit.

But today, the sight of you in jumbo rounds
piled carelessly around the stump
and the enormous space that has opened up
over the land you governed,
I feel a twinge of emptiness, of angst really,
your reddish dust covering the lawn and patio,
your sweet organic fragrance lingering.

OLD MAN WINTER
after William Stafford (1914-1993)

A late winter snow
Sudden deep and wet
The boughs all bent
The witchhazel spent.

Pink blossoms—
Whitcombii cherry,
Cilpenese—
Peeking through white.

When my time comes
I hope to go
Like this old man,
Air shimmering bright.

WALKING IN THE WOODS WITHOUT AN iPHONE

—the red crest of pileated woodpeckers their drumming the whinnying flight of the flicker its white rump the call of the owl the eagle and the quail the basket bark of cedar the insipid taste of salmonberries the wild huckleberry's tartness licorice fern rooted in the bark of big-leaf maple the purplish blush of alder its hanging catkins the Indian plum its white blossoms the leathery leaves of salal the yellow flowers of Oregon grape the fragrance of evergreen after rain.

CEDAR STUMPS

There are other reminders of our past: the native ferns:
wood, sword, deer, lady, licorice;
and the wild flowers, the vines, the shrubs, the berries;
and of course the other trees:
the fir, the spruce, the hemlock, the yew, the deciduous.
But it's the stumps of ancient cedar
fallen a century ago, persevered in their organic oils,
that have survived as reminders
of our forefather's conquest of the forests.
Many stumps nurse seedlings, some expose notches
cut into their flanks, notches
that held springboards on which lumberjacks stood
pulling crosscut saws back and forth,
                              until the giants were felled.

OCEANSPRAY

You must have noticed those large shrubs
covered with clusters of creamy-white flowers
that festoon our roadways in early summer?

But have you ever paused to examine one's
serrated green leaves, or bend over a bloom
to breathe in its subtle fragrance?

Native Americans called the shrub Ironwood
after the hardness of its wood;
made of it needles, hooks and nails.

Oceanspray speaks from our town's deep past,
but if you are alive to the present
you may see a deer nibble its leaves,
or later, clinging to a tattered, decaying cluster,
a bird surviving on its seeds.

SENSUALITY

My lacecap hydrangea envelops a six foot stone sculpture.
It leafs out in spring and flowers in late summer.

It is strikingly pleasing to the eye. Its flowers:
purple seed pods fringed with white petals, adorn the shrub.

But it's the large elliptical green leaves with a hint of down
that awaken my desire to touch.

SUNDAY MORNINGS

He rides past turns around
drives back.
I think he's lost his way.

No, no he says,
I'm Dr. Hahn, a physician.
I teach wellness at the
Korean church.

He asks if we always pick up
litter on Sunday.
Every morning, my wife says.

He wants to teach caring,
asks if he can use our names.

No problem I say,
but under what session,
mind, body or spirit?

Oh, spirit he says. In that case
—needing extra credit, I say,
we also hand out treats
to friendly dogs.

PAVAROTTI ON SUNSET AVENUE

My wife and I like living here
in this new apartment building
above the beach, the ferry terminal,
and the train tracks.
Fog horns and train whistles suit us.
The walk north is pleasant
—beach roses on the beach side
and private homes
with trim lawns and flower gardens
on the other.

The people we meet in the morning
walking dogs are friendly.
Most of the drivers stay in their cars
reading, listening to music, news.
some are out looking
over the Sound toward the Olympics,
some taking photos

In late afternoons and early evenings
couples or singles,
with or without dogs or children,
stroll by our apartment on Bell street
to unwind, watch the sun set.
One would be hard pressed to find
despair on these streets.

                              But I know
there are a few in tight quarters,
unable to maneuver,
questioning their strength to go on.
I know this because I too drove here,
in times past,
listening to Pavarotti, restoring hope.

LUNCH AT GIRARDI'S

When Robert Penn Warren was dying and was asked
if he possessed any religious convictions
that might bring him comfort in his hard last hours he said,
No, I don't have any religious beliefs. I always assumed
that my lack of belief was a shortcoming,
                    like my inability to appreciate music.

When Richard Wilbur was criticized for his rosy view of life
he replied, I feel that the universe is full of glorious energy
tending to take pattern and shape,
and that the ultimate character of things is comely and good.
I am perfectly aware
that I say this in the teeth of all sorts of contrary evidence
and that I must be basing it partly
                    on temperament and partly on faith.

When, last week, having lunch with two old colleagues,
the one who had recently lost his wife
                    asked if I believe in Heaven.
I should have explained it this way:
In thirty years of making poems in response to the subjects
and questions that presented themselves
I have realized a tenderness for this dusty world
                    and have no need or want of another.

THIS WORLD IS THE OTHER WORLD
for Chris

You express full agreement with this line
in one of my nature poems,
noting that, *Heaven's right here before our eyes.*

But when I send you this quote from Hume:
*It is a most unreasonable fancy
that we should exist forever,* you plead

ignorance concerning the old philosophers.
Instead, you opine: *For the moment,
watching wind blow leaves around the yard
                    seems pretty fulfilling.*

ROMNEYA POPPIES
for Ed

It's fine for Ruskin to criticize sentimentality in poetry calling it the "pathetic fallacy," or for Keats to claim that a man of achievement is capable of facing doubts without any irritable reaching after facts and reasons,

Still, here I am applauding Ed's Romneya poppies as lovely dancers, imagining their petals as white skirts billowing in the breeze and their seed pods as orange hats, a most enjoyable and non-intrusive means of subduing dread.

MODES OF SURVIAL
for Ralph

From where I'm resting on a green metal bench,
looking out over the waters of Puget Sound,
        I watch the struggle to live in full fury
—thirty or more gulls are plundering
what I think may be an injured seal or dolphin.
But when a neighbor stops by
—we are both out on our early morning walk,
he tells me it's a herring ball.
           Never heard of such a thing, I say.
I do know that herring sweep the sea in schools
—sheltering single members,
               as they search for food.
But, he tells me, when the auklet
—a seabird evolved to dive deep and fast,
            come upon a school,
they herd it up to surface as the stronger fish
        fight into the center to save the species.

Then my neighbor asks, if I'll be home later
—he wants to fetch us a mess of French beans.
He tells me they are so sweet.
    In *sotto voce*, he says, I'm kinda proud of them.

NOTES

Old Man Winter,
    after William Stafford's lines:
      If I die, I'd like to die
      in the evening. That way, I'll have
      all the dark to go with me, and no one
      will see how I begin to hobble along

Lunch at Girardi's,
    Robert Penn Warren (1905-1989)
      U. S. Poet Laureate, 1944
      Pulitzer Prize for fiction, 1947
      Pulitzer Prize for poetry. 1957, 1979

    Richard Wilbur (1921-2017)
      Pulitzer Prize for poetry, 1957
      U. S. Poet Laureate, 1987

This World Is the Other World,
    David Hume (1711-1776) Moral Philosopher

Romneya Poppies,
    John Ruskin (1819-1900) Art Critic
    John Keats (1795-1821) Romantic Poet

www.ingramcontent.com/pod-product-compliance
Lightning Source LLC
LaVergne TN
LVHW051610080426
835510LV00020B/3214